# This book belongs to

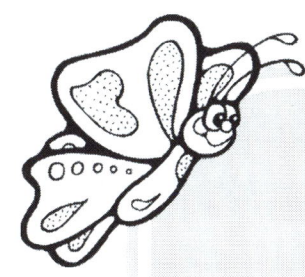

Claireoorathybrewer

# a

a a a a a a a a
a a a a a a a a a

# and

and and and and and
and and and and and

# away

away away away away
away away away away

# big

big big big big big big
big big big big big big

3

# blue

blue blue blue blue blue
blue blue blue blue

# can

can I go to the
stor store store store
store store

# come

with
come whith me.
With with with

# down

please sit
plese set down. please
pleas Please please
sit sit sit sit

# find

You can find it by your self. your your your your your your

# for

This is for you.

# funny

you are funny.

# go

you can go fast.

# help

I need help.

# here

I am here.

# i

I am going now.

# in

I am going in.

## is

Ite is hard*ing hard.

## it

It is small.

# jump

I can Jump.

# little

you are little.

# look

Look by me.

# make

I make it.

## me

Me and you are my
frens. *(friends)* friends friends friends

friends friends friends

## my  cut / cute

My Mommy is cut.

Cute cute cute cute

cute cute cute cute cute

## not

Do not climb the mountain
Monte
with out
whie ot Mommy and Daddy.

climb mountain with out

## one

Know — With
Know how how spanish

I now whow to say
          Spanish    with
one in Spenesh wet out

help with my Mom and dad.

# play

I play all day.

# red

I have a red cray.

# run

I run fast.

# said

I said Hi to my Mom.

# see

See the tree.

# the

The tree is tall.

# three

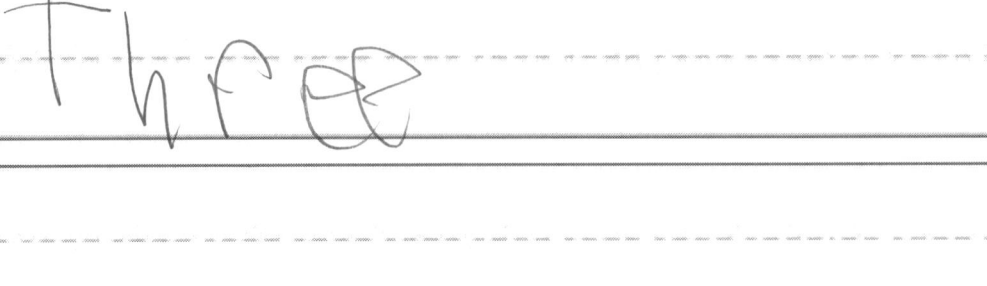

# to

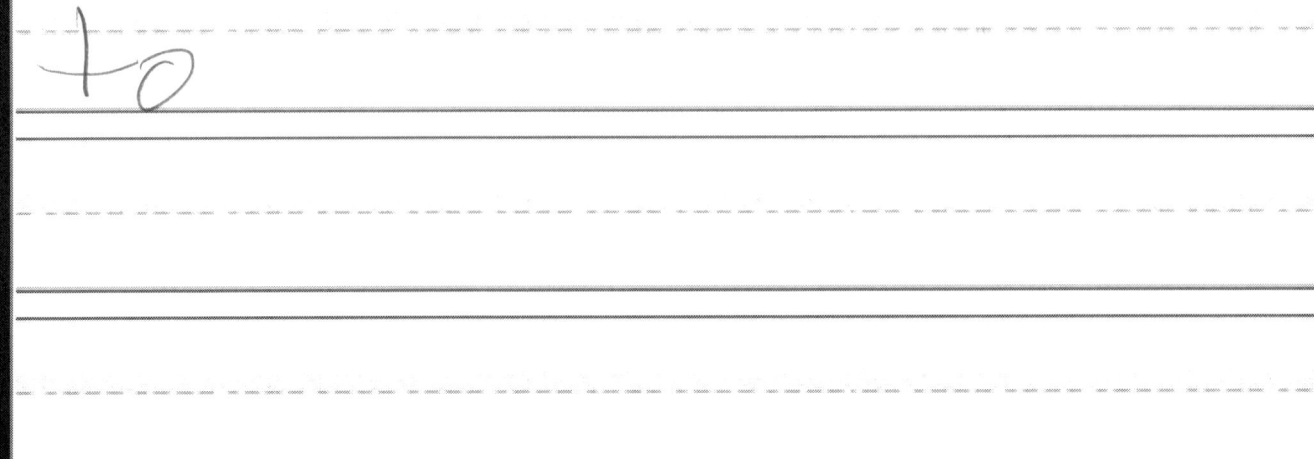

two

two

up

up

# we

we

# where

where

# yellow

Yellow

# you

you

# all

all

# am

am

# are

are

# at

at

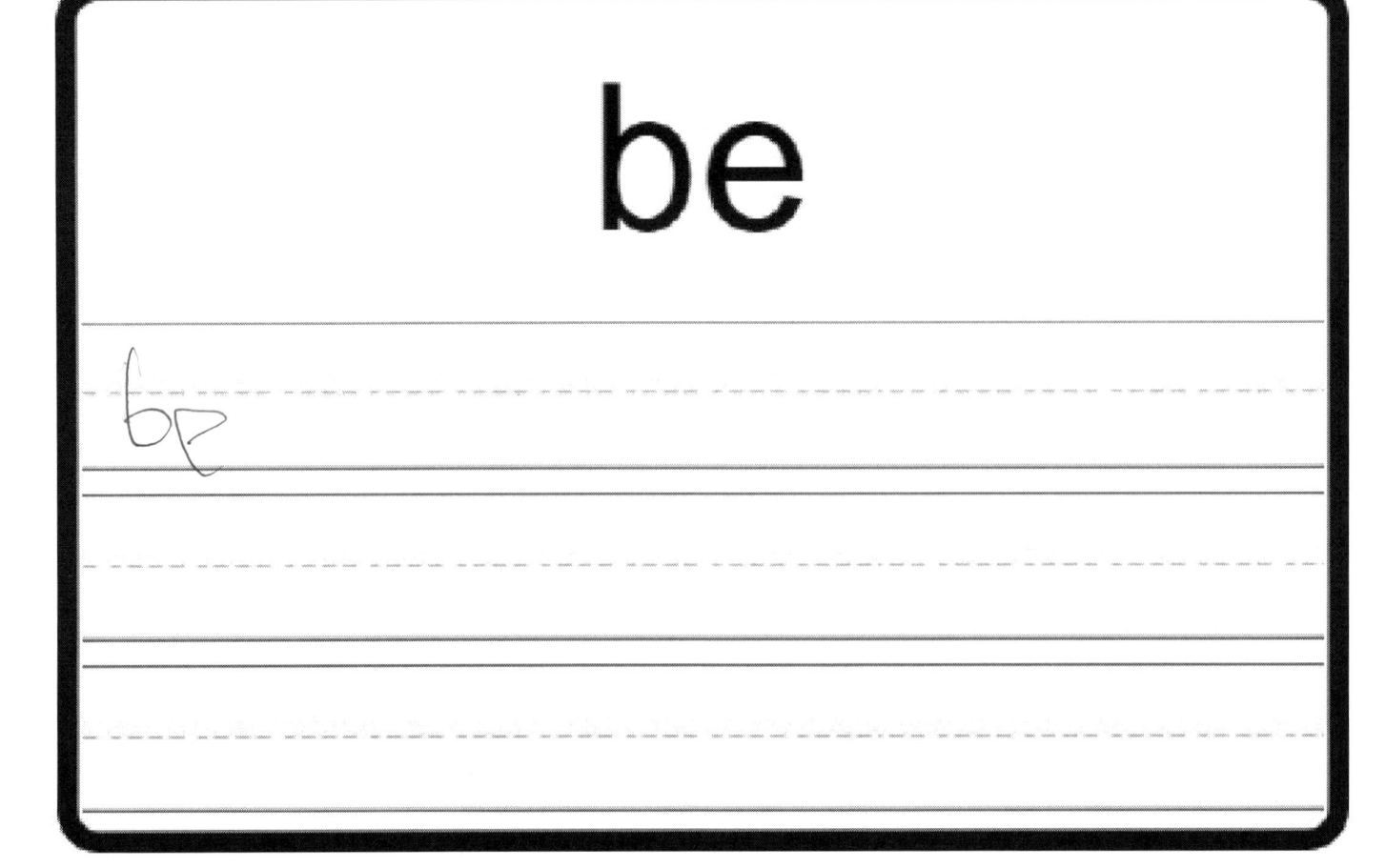

# ate

*ate*

# be

*be*

# black

black

# brown

brown

# but

*but*

# came

*came*

# did

did

# do

do

eat

eat

four

four

# get

get

# good

good

## have

have

## he

he

15

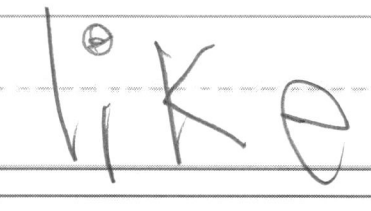

# into

into

# like

like

# must

must

# new

new

# no

no

# now

now

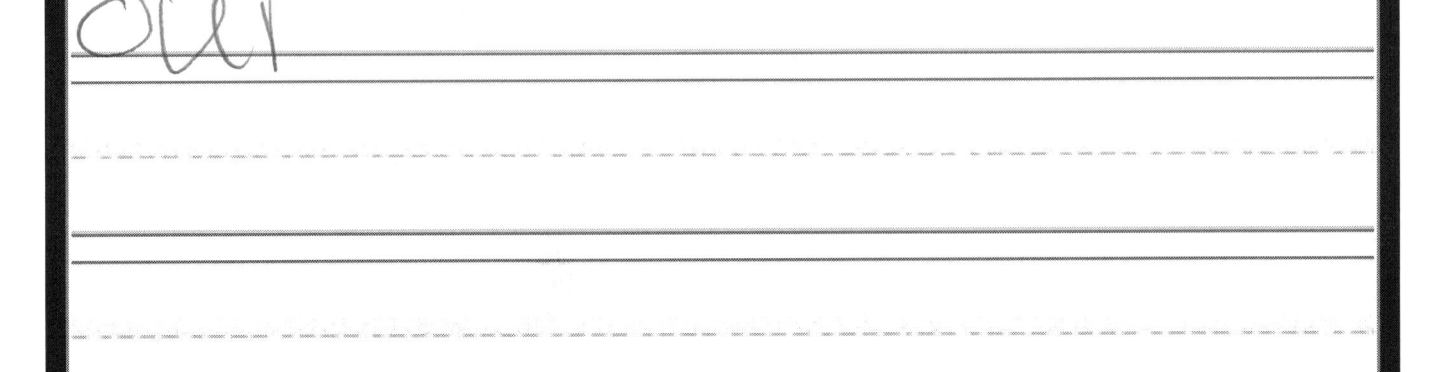

# on

on

# our

our

4

## out

a u

## please

please

## pretty

phvetty

## ran

ran

# ride

*ride*

# saw

say

she

so

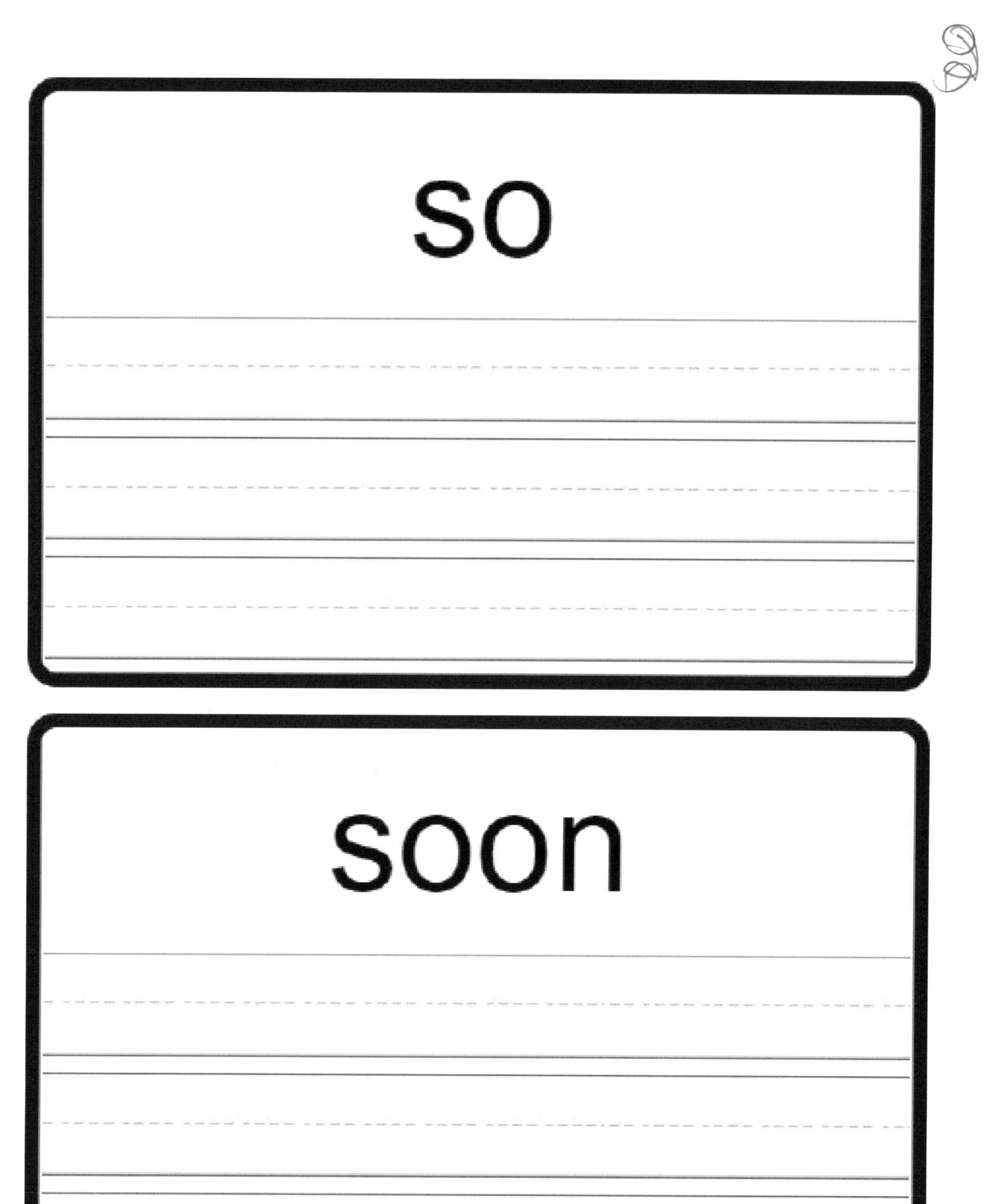

soon

that

there

# they

# this

too

under

want

was

well

went

what

white

who

will

with

yes

after

again

an

any

as

ask

by

could

every

fly

# from

# give

# going

# had

has

her

him

his

how

just

know

let

live

may

of

old

once

open

over

put

# round

# some

# stop

# take

thank

them

then

think

walk

were

when

always

# around

# because

been

before

best

both

buy

call

cold

does

don't

fast

# first

# five

found

gave

# goes

# green

its

made

many

off

or

pull

# read

# right

sing

sit

# sleep

# tell

# their

# these

those

upon

us

use

very

wash

which

why

wish

work

# would

# write

your

about

better

bring

carry

clean

cut

done

# draw

# drink

# eight

# fall

far

full

# got

# grow

hold

hot

hurt

if

# keep

# kind

laugh

light

long

much

myself

never

only

own

# pick

# seven

shall

show

# six

# small

# start

# ten

today

together

try

warm

Made in the USA
Columbia, SC
03 June 2020